EVERYONE NEEDS A

SAM

THE ONES
STANDING BESIDE YOU
AND GUARDING YOUR BACK.
MENTORS FOR LIFE.

Everyone Needs a SAM
ISBN: 978-0-88144-244-1
Copyright © 2010 by John A. Winters

Published by
Total Publishing and Media
9731 East 54th Street
Tulsa, OK 74146
www.totalpublishingandmedia.com

WHAT OTHERS ARE
SAYING ABOUT "SAM"

John Winters has provided a key to open doors to personal peace and success. As business professionals, athletes or just as men, greater accomplishments can be achieved by trusting the advice of our mentors, or "Sams", as Winters calls them.

My personal success as an SEC record holder in track is partially due to my coach, who was an Olympic Gold medalist. The difference in first and second place was achieved by following the instruction and guidance of one who had been there.

Winters has a winner with his book. He has written an amazing and thought provoking read, citing personal experiences. The author challenges us to evaluate our direction, rely on others' wisdom and the power of prayer to discover what we can become.

KERMIT PERRY
Former Assistant Athletics Director
University of Georgia and Auburn University

After reading "Everyone Needs A Sam," I now have a new word for "true friends," that being a SAM."

My wife of 21 years, Ceann, and I have been blessed with numerous SAMS, including John and Corby Winters. Further, the love of God, family and SAMS has been a large part of our lives and successful marriage.

So I have to ask, "Do you have a SAM?" If not, why not? You are only one SAM away from having a "true friend."

"Everyone Needs A Sam" is not only motivational and inspirational, but a great read.

DAVE BURLEW
Special Agent
Federal Bureau of Investigation

John Winters has captured in "Everyone Needs a Sam" the essence of each individual's longing for support. Not necessarily friendship, or even mentoring, but something deeper and more vital: He called this "our Sam". I invite you to read and discover for yourself how to find yours.

JERRY TOOPS, Ph.D., LCSW
Director of Healing
First United Methodist Church
Tulsa, Oklahoma

Everyone Needs A Sam was such an inspiring book to me. In dealing for the past 11 years in Men's Ministry, I have seen the need for men to be connected and mentored. As I was reading this my mind went back to the many men that have been there for me and have been "my Sams." Just as John points out, some are still in that roll and some have moved on, but these encounters have shown me how valuable they were in my life.

I am now in a season of my life where God has placed me in the role of a Sam to several men that I am either serving with or in a leadership role over. Each day I see how God can use each one of us to help those around us with words of wisdom, a helping hand, or just by being there. I see the importance of showing up in their lives just as others have been there for me.

I am so thrilled with this book and thank you John for your obedience to God to write it. John brings out numerous truths in this work and I believe it will inspire many others to be a Sam. I look forward to reading about your account of the Sams in your life!

TY BARKER
Director of Men's Ministry and
Co-Pastor of Victory Singles
Victory Christian Center
Tulsa, Oklahoma

I read "Everyone Needs A Sam" with great interest and found it to be insightful and compelling.

We all certainly need our Sams who can help guide us through our lives. Sams who can give us sound advice to help us avoid the pitfalls and to make the right decisions, which lead us to true success and happiness. How blessed we are when we find the Ultimate Sam ... the one who has never made a mistake and whose wisdom and direction is always perfect regarding our decisions in life.

John places the proper emphasis and reliance upon Scriptures and his final chapter shows a clear and concise offer to finding the Ultimate Sam.

DOUG MOBLEY
Douglas L. Mobley Foundation

DEDICATION

To all the Sams that were,
that are and that will be.

And to the Little Black Dress,
my favorite Sam.

TABLE OF CONTENTS

ACKNOWLEDGEMENTS

In another section of this book I discuss how you should never start a thank-you list, because you are going to forget someone.

Nevertheless, I will do my best.

I spent more than 24 years in the newspaper industry, most of that time as a journalist and editor. If I've learned anything, it's that you can never edit yourself.

To Jean and Brenda Hendryx, Julie and Keith Martin, Carol Sanders, Betsy Perry and Ed and Cynthia Hunt — thank you for taking the time to add your comments and being incredibly gracious in your edits.

To my parents, Otis and Ann Winters, who remained steadfast in their support while I was trying to figure out the next phase of my life. They were probably more excited about this project than anyone, and that meant a great deal. And they were, and are, my original Sams.

To all the Sams in my life — too many to count — thank you. You will meet a few of them later in the book, but there are many, many more out there. Without you, there would be no book and my life would not be what it is.

To the Sons of Thunder — Caleb, Seth and Levi — my boys. Thanks for putting up with me and giving me space while "dad's working on his book." You are an incredible gift. My prayer and hope is to always be your Sam and that you continue being Sams to each other and anyone who asks.

To the Little Black Dress, my wife, what can I say? Thank you for your amazing support, and your sweet, yet insistent persistence to "write the book." Your belief in me and your prayers are the reason this book exists.

And finally, to the Ultimate Sam; sorry it took so long.

FOREWORD

People are made for relationship.

In Genesis 2:18, God saw that it was not good for Adam to be alone, so He created Eve. Life should be lived in community. We need each other whether it is family, friends, co-workers, neighbors, or just casual acquaintances. We need love. We need support.

One Sunday John Winters, his wife, and two "Sons of Thunder" appeared at my church (the youngest son was not yet born). Soon, they were part of our church family. When one of us celebrated, just like the rest of the church family, the Winters celebrated too. When one of us struggled, they struggled with us. As their pastor, it was my privilege to officiate the renewal of their marriage vows and baptize the youngest "Son of Thunder" after his arrival.

John is one of those people you can count on. Unlike John, I'm not really a golfer, but I thought it would be fun to try, so I asked John to take me with him. John patiently endured my embarrassing shots and faithfully drove the golf cart to retrieve my golf ball from the most ridiculous places. Any number of things could have been said about my lack of skills at the game, but John made no such remarks. In fact, he was more than gracious.

For John, this kindness and graciousness is natural, so it comes as no surprise that he would write a book like "Everyone Needs a Sam." He has shown me, and has shown many others, what a true Sam looks like, and will show you in the following pages.

My greatest claim to fame is that God called me to be a pastor. At the time it seemed to be an impossible calling. Sometimes it still does. Graciously, and thankfully, God didn't expect me to answer His call without real support from a lot of people — a lot of Sams.

I wish I had had this book at the time. Looking back on those early years in ministry; the long hours studying, the occasional useless seminary class, the sermons that didn't convey exactly what I had hoped, and the many mistakes, I see the faces of some of those who helped me. If I had had the wisdom presented in "Everyone Needs A Sam," I would have better recognized my Sams for what they were. I would have been more intentional to celebrate the victories with them.

Sometimes Sams just happen. You need one, and one appears from nowhere. In such cases, they are a Godsend. In this book, John Winters reminds us that life is not lived in isolation. He opens the reader's eyes to recognize people who have helped carry their burdens and inspires them to help others who are burdened.

Between the covers of this book you will find wisdom and inspiration from the author's personal reflections as well as a collection of stories and testimonies from those who have supported and influenced others.

"Everyone Needs A Sam," so as you read, take the time to reflect on the Sams in your life, then write your own story. Take the opportunity and the time to go back and thank those who supported you when you needed it most. As you celebrate the Sams of your past, look forward to the Sams of your future. In addition, discover how you can be a Sam.

Everyone needs a Sam, but most importantly everyone needs the Ultimate Sam. Now, it's time for you to hear from John Winters and the Ultimate Sam.

JOHN W. FREELAND
Pastor
Skyland United Methodist Church
Atlanta, Georgia

AUTHOR'S NOTE

Everyone Needs A Sam focuses on finding those unique individuals in life who help guide your path. Known as "Sams," they also could be considered guides, friends, mentors or counselors.

Yet at their core, Sams are living "wisdom," as viewed from a Biblical perspective. They speak the truth, they stand by you, they watch your back. Some Sams are in your life forever, others only for a particular instance.

This book discusses the various types of Sams, how to find them, what they are and are not, and also their limitations. It concludes with finding the "Ultimate Sam."

Although *Everyone Needs A Sam* is written from a man's perspective, I hope women will apply it as well. This book is useful for those just starting out on their life journey with first jobs, marriage and new families. Yet it is also valuable to individuals in their 40s and 50s, especially those facing job loss and other economic hardships.

I wrote this as a first-person account of my own experiences. I spent more than 24 years in the newspaper industry, was publisher of a daily newspaper and was later out of work for more than a year. Throughout my career, and to this day, I've had Sams. And I illustrate the positive impacts these people had on my life and what I learned from them.

The second part of this book includes vignettes from various people who helped me at different points in my life. These vignettes, known as "Sams on Sams," are about these men and women who had someone help them at some time. Their own stories, so to speak.

The final section includes a web site where I invite you to go and write about your own Sams. I hope you will celebrate your mentors, those individuals who took the time to help you.

Everyone needs a Sam. And everyone needs to be a Sam to someone else.

If you don't know which way to turn, then this book is for you. If you want to change the world, even if it's only one person at a time, then this book is for you.

Be a Sam.

PART ONE

CHAPTER ONE

THE SAM

"The next best thing to being wise oneself
is to live in a circle of those who are"
—C.S. Lewis

"Getting wisdom is the wisest thing you can do!
And whatever else you do,
develop good judgment."

PROVERBS 4:7

There are times in life when we need direction. We've hit that wall. We need help. And we just don't know which way to go.

That's where a Sam comes in. Usually, you have to go and find one; sometimes they find you. Sams can appear when you least expect them, or didn't even know you needed one. But you discover you're glad they did.

Everyone needs a Sam.

At times a Sam might be a mentor. Other times it's that person who is just there, sitting beside you while you face those life demons. And sometimes they are a real thorn in the flesh, because they're yanking you out of your comfort zone.

They have various roles: counselor, friend, mentor, sounding board, the one guarding your back, and sometimes your front. The one the Bible calls "wisdom." That's a Sam.

Let's be clear. They are not angels, at least real angels. And they're not some cosmic force helping to get your karma in order. They are real, just like you, and you need them.

The idea of the strong, silent individual who needs no one is best found in fiction or the movies. No one does it all on his own. Everyone has someone at some point in their life, whether they realize it or not.

A Sam might be your spouse — sometimes. They might be your best friend, but not always. These individuals may come and go; others stay for a lifetime.

They are the ones who stand by you when everyone else has deserted. They speak the truth in your life when no one else will. They walk with you to the mountaintop and share your joy there; but also walk with you through your deepest valley and share your deepest pain.

It's important to remember that Sams are human. And in the end, they can only do so much. At some point, it's up to you, because a true Sam is not a crutch.

One of my favorite books of all time is *The Lord of the Rings* by J.R.R. Tolkien. What always struck me, besides the great battles of course, were the incredible bonds between the main characters. They always stood up for each other, defended each other, and took care of each other.

I always wanted to write about that.

There is a scene near the end of the last book where the hero, Frodo, and his best friend, Sam, are trying to get inside Mount Doom. Their mission is to throw a magical ring of pure evil that Frodo has carried throughout the three-book series into the fire to destroy it and save Middle Earth.

In this scene, Frodo collapses on the mountainside, he can't go any farther. Their long, dangerous journey has failed. Evil will take over Middle Earth.

Sam is also spent, but he refuses to give up. He looks at Frodo and says, "Come, Mr. Frodo. I can't carry it for you, but I can carry you … Sam will give you a ride. Just tell him where to go, and he'll go." And then Sam picks up Frodo and starts to climb Mount Doom.

Not long ago, I remember watching the movie version with my wife, affectionately known as the Little Black Dress. I turned to her and said "Everyone needs a Sam."

And she looked at me and said, "Write the book."

And so I did.

A Sam can't carry your burden, but he can carry you.

I am blessed. I have Sams, and I hope to meet more in the future. They stand with me; they tell me the truth; they guard my back. When I simply don't know what to do, where to turn, they show up. They will be among those who have the greatest impact in your life. Cherish them.

Everyone needs a Sam.

Let's go find yours.

CHAPTER TWO

SAMS COME AND GO

"Some people come into our lives and quickly go.
Some stay for a while, leave footprints on
our hearts, and we are never, ever the same."
—Flavia Weedn

*"The godly give good advice to their friends;
the wicked lead them astray."*

PROVERBS 12:26

Some Sams are with you a long time; others
appear, give their wisdom, and disappear.

I was giving a speech at our annual corporate meeting.
After I finished and during a break, one of the corporate

bigwigs came up to me, took me aside and said I had really insulted another colleague with my comments.

I had no idea and it certainly wasn't my intention. And I seriously had to think long and hard about what it was I said that was offensive. How could I have been misunderstood? I knew in my gut this corporate guy was right. So I sought out the other executive and apologized.

I doubt I ever really salvaged that relationship with the man who took offense, but at least I tried. And the only reason I apologized was because this Sam had just appeared. The kicker is this man was the kind who would close down the bar; a total party guy. For the record, no, he was not a Christian and not the kind of person you'd recommend as a Sam. But for that one moment, he was mine. He was there for me.

Some Sams are in your life forever. Some pop up out of nowhere, hit you with whatever, and disappear. At those times, you probably didn't even think about it — or them. It's not until later you realize their impact on you.

But they've long since gone and you never really thanked them. It's something that just blows past you and you're like, "whoa, what was that?"

Some Sams come and go.

And I've found it's those people who often have a bigger and immediate impact. They are there for a season, maybe a single event. They're those people who pass through your life at exactly the right moment. Are you open enough to recognize this Sam when you meet him?

Those of us trying to walk the walk believe God brings these men and women into our lives. Many times they serve as a brake; other times a gut-check that what you just did — or are about to do — needs to be rethought.

God uses people. He uses people of all walks and every status. He brings people into our lives at times for specific purposes. And these Sams aren't always Christians.

One of my greatest Sams was no Bible-thumper. At one time I worked for him, later in my career we were peers running affiliated companies. While we were separated by many states running our respective companies, this guy dropped more pearls of wisdom on me than anyone else in my career.

We'd bump into each other at some meeting or just have a chance phone call. Almost every time, at some point he'd pull out "you might want to think about that."

Bam. And he was right every time.

These Sams aren't always your peers; not always your best friends. And that's simply because they come and go. You might work with them for a while, you might live near them at some point or see them at church or your kid's school. But they, or you, move on.

I believe these are some of the most powerful influences you will have in your life. And as I said earlier, often you don't realize they were Sams until after the fact.

The question is how do you know whether these individuals are true Sams? The answer is they have nothing to gain. They are not playing sides, trying to get you to somehow fulfill their own agenda. Truth be told, many times they'd be better off if they didn't say anything.

There is nothing in it for them — if one looks at it from the world's viewpoint. But for some reason, they appear. They say what they need to say and then they are gone. To paraphrase an old Southern expression, "they don't have a dog in the hunt."

We need to be careful, because everyone is more than willing to offer advice. And if you're facing a major decision that impacts a lot of people, you'll get lots of advice. The majority of that advice is slanted to benefit the one giving the advice.

"Only simpletons believe everything they're told! The prudent carefully consider their steps. The wise are cautious and avoid danger; fools plunge ahead with reckless confidence." (Proverbs 14: 15-16)

In my own life, these Sams came in all ages and sizes. Yet I've found the vast majority of them are older than I am. I don't know why, yet I've come to value — and trust — the opinions and suggestions they give more. Maybe it's an age thing, or a "been there, done that," life experience.

It's interesting that the Bible also points out the value of wisdom and advice from older generations. The Bible shows what can happen when one ignores the advice of those who have already faced similar situations.

Solomon was the third king of the united Israel in biblical times. During his reign, Israel was at its height in terms of power and riches. Upon his death, his son Rehoboam took power. And it was at this time that the Israelites approached the new young king to ask that their tax burdens be eased.

Rehoboam talked to his father's advisers. And then he talked to his friends. The older men had fought their battles, they had no more dragons to slay. The king's friends wanted power and money. The older men suggested Rehoboam reduce the taxes to keep the peace and the country united. The friends urged him to increase taxes; surely no ulterior motive there.

"But Rehoboam rejected the advice of the older men and instead asked the opinion of the young men who had grown up with him and were now his advisers." (I Kings 12:8)

The result? Civil war and the once great nation split into two separate countries. And Rehoboam was left with about a tenth of what he once had to govern.

Rehoboam had the chance to listen to his father's advisors, men who helped build the greatest country in the world at the time. He chose not listen to them. And so those counselors left.

Some Sams come and go. The key is to listen while they are still there.

You may or may not realize them at the time they appear. But you will know them because they were right and they had nothing to gain.

While some Sams are for a season, others are around for the long haul, a lifetime. Those are the ones we call friends, best friends. They are the ones who know us better than anyone. When you think about it, what better Sams are there than the ones we hang around with?

Shouldn't our best friends be our Sams? Sometimes, but not always.

CHAPTER THREE

A SAM IS NOT ALWAYS YOUR BEST FRIEND

"It is one of the blessings of old friends that
you can afford to be stupid with them."
Ralph Waldo Emerson

"Many will say they are loyal friends,
but who can find one who is truly reliable?"
PROVERBS 20:6

You can tell a lot about a person by their friends.

Next to your spouse, your friends have the greatest
impact on your life. It's just the way it is — the people

you hang around with are the ones that will influence you the most.

I realize this is not a new revelation for many of you, but sometimes we forget. That's especially true for those of you, like me, raising kids like Caleb, Seth and Levi; our version of the Sons of Thunder. And yes, it's what our parents drilled into us — you are your friends. My parents were always checking out my friends and I knew when they did not approve of someone. They made it very clear.

And now I'm doing the exact same thing my parents did. And there are times my sons are not too happy with my decisions. Life repeats itself. And my parents were right, and sometimes that's a hard pill for us to swallow ... you know, admitting our parents were right.

In this chapter, I'm not talking about acquaintances or friends. I'm talking those individuals we classify as best friends. The ones we grew up with. The ones who stand beside you when you get married, whispering in your ear not to lock your knees. The ones you call in the middle of the night for whatever reason and they drive miles to be there.

And for many guys, they are the ones you had that first underage beer with out in the woods. The ones standing beside you sheepishly while your parents give you the "what were you thinking?!" lecture. Those kinds of friends.

I don't know about you, but I'll admit I've had a lot of friends like that — much to my parents' consternation.

Let's face it, if you ever got in trouble, I'll take the bet your best friends were around. In Proverbs, the author states "as iron sharpens iron, so a friend sharpens a friend." (27:17). And that can be good or bad.

We need to surround ourselves with godly friends. And those types of friends can be Sams. "The godly give good advice to their friends; the wicked lead them astray." (Proverbs 12:26). We need those kinds of friends, those kinds of Sams.

Your best friend can be a Sam. But it's imperative that friend be a true and godly individual. "There are 'friends' who destroy each other, but a real friend sticks closer than a brother." (Proverbs 18:24).

Our best friends often times know things about us that our spouses don't. They are about as close to being a spouse as you can get. They know all your stuff. Unfortunately, sometimes they are closer than your spouse. And that's not a good thing. If that's the case, your priorities are wrong, because that means there's something you're hiding.

Your spouse should be No. 1. You are allowed only a few secrets from your spouse — things like the surprise two-week vacation trip to Hawaii you've promised for 10 years.

Your friends are your Sams. The issue is whether they should be. The deciding factor is simple. The Bible says "wounds from a sincere friend are better than many kisses from an enemy," (Proverbs 27:6) and "the heartfelt counsel of a friend is as sweet as perfume and incense." (Proverbs 27:9).

If you can read those two scriptures and say, "yep, that's Tom," then Tom is a Sam. If not, get a new friend. Real friends, real Sams, are going to hold you accountable. They are going to tell you the truth. To borrow from Proverbs 17:17, "a 'Sam' is always loyal."

The key is that they are loyal to your best interests. They are not loyal to your stupidity or your decision to do wrong. They are not going to play your game. A true Sam is going to say "no" more than they will say "yes." And they will fight you, risk that friendship, to keep you on the right path.

Many men will tell you their best friend is their wife. I remember vividly one time when my wife, the Little Black Dress, looked at me and said, "we're not best friends are we?"

And I looked right at her and said, "No."

She recounted this story later to the women who attended her weekly Bible study. I'm sure there were a few gasps and "oh, they must be having serious marital problems" comments. But then The Dress smiled at everyone and said, "but he told me he would die for me."

And I guess I scored some points because The Dress later told me there were a few heads nodding and a few tears shed among the women.

It might just be a question of semantics, that definition of a best friend. I don't see her as my best friend, but I do see her as my best Sam.

To me, my best friend is beside me out in the freezing cold with rain pouring down horizontally out in the middle of a river waving a stick. Or fly fishing if you prefer.

The Little Black Dress is known as a fair weather fly fisherman(woman). She's good when the sun is out, there's no wind and there's lots of salmon. And she's done after an hour. Honestly, I'd rather fly fish with my wife, but I just like to fish for more than an hour and regardless of the weather.

I also practice catch-and-release, a concept foreign to the Little Black Dress. She simply doesn't understand the point. To her, you fish to catch fish and then eat them.

Of course, The Dress sees best friends as those who will travel miles to find that one pair of shoes, and then fawn over them for days. And that's a concept foreign to me.

My wife is more than my best friend. She's me. "This explains why a man leaves his father and mother and is joined to his wife, and the two are united into one." (Genesis 2:24)

The Bible says "There is no greater love than to lay down one's life for one's friends." (John 15:13).

I don't know if I'm there yet. For the Little Black Dress, yes. For my friends? Well, it's easy to sit here at a computer and pontificate on how we'd just follow that scripture all the way to heaven. Easy to say.

But I will say this. A real Sam will do that. And there's a real man who's already done that for you. You'll meet him later.

So your best friend may not always be your best Sam. Fortunately, at least you've got your spouse — right?

Right?

CHAPTER FOUR

A SAM IS NOT ALWAYS YOUR SPOUSE

"My most brilliant achievement was my ability
to be able to persuade my wife to marry me."
—Winston Churchill

"Who can find a virtuous and capable wife?
She is more precious than rubies."

PROVERBS 31:10

There's very little I wouldn't tell the Little Black Dress. And yet, she is not always my Sam.

Before we delve into this section, there's a caveat: you have to like your spouse; you have to love him or her; and you have to respect each other. Otherwise, drop this book and immediately seek counsel. Come back when you've got your marriage where it needs to be.

In a perfect world, your spouse would be your Sam. No one should support you like your spouse. They are the ones you can — and should — turn to. Let's face it, they know you better than anyone else.

They know your strengths and they know your weaknesses. They know what moves you and what ticks you off. They are a part of your highest highs and your lowest lows. They are you.

And therein lies the problem.

I could not ask for a better Sam than the Little Black Dress. Though "the grass withers and the flowers fall" (I Peter 1:25), The Dress stands by me. Though "Mountains will be thrown down; cliffs will crumble; walls will fall to the earth" (Ezekiel 38:20), The Dress is always there.

I am fortunately … very fortunate.

And therein lies the problem.

I know the Little Black Dress will always support me. I know she will always have my back so to speak. I know she will give me the best advice she can knowing what all she knows — about the situation and about me.

And too often I go "yeah, yeah." And that's simply because I know she's there. I know she has my best interests at heart. And I hear it a lot. It's not that her opinion doesn't carry weight, because it does, more than anyone else.

The contradiction is simple. Your spouse should be your Sam. But sometimes we just need an outside source. Maybe it's because we sometimes get overloaded with all that spousal support. We (hopefully) get so much we just come to expect it.

I know my wife is my biggest supporter. But sometimes, I need to hear it from someone else. Sometimes, not always, I need another validation. And that last sentence raises the question: Why? Why do we need to hear from someone other than the one who cares about us more than anyone?

We just do.

The ones that really matter — our spouses, our greatest support system — are the very ones we ignore at times. And so we continue to piddle and mope while our spouse is banging us over the head with the "wake-up, reality check, listen to me because I love you, you can do this, I believe in you," golf club.

But despite all the positive reinforcement, the truth is, sometimes we just need another voice. Someone not quite as close. Someone with a different perspective. Someone whose interest in us follows another path. Someone who might have a wider lens, or at least a different zoom.

Enter Sam.

And a Sam is just going to see things differently. They (usually) don't pick up your underwear, change your sheets and tell you, yet again, to take out the trash. That's called a maid. And yes, sometimes a spouse.

This Sam is not your spouse. How they relate to you is simply different. And because of that, sometimes their voice carries significant weight.

There's nothing wrong with seeking counsel — the Bible encourages it. "Plans succeed through good counsel; don't go to war without wise advice." (Proverbs 20:18).

The book of Proverbs is full of advice; advice from the wisest man who ever lived. When Solomon was made king of Israel, the Bible tells us God asked him what he wanted. Think about that — this was no genie in the bottle offering a series of wishes. This was the God of the universe basically offering Solomon a blank check.

The Bible never says what was going on in Solomon's mind when God made the offer. Reading the verses in question, it's almost like the king responded right away. I have a feeling, however, that Solomon took his time and really thought about it. And his wish? — wisdom.

"The Lord was pleased that Solomon had asked for wisdom. So God replied, "Because you have asked for wisdom in governing my people with justice and have not asked for a long life or wealth or the death of your enemies — I will give you what you have asked for! I will give you a wise and understanding heart such as no one else has had or ever will have." (I Kings 3:10-12).

We would be wise to listen to a man whom God has endowed with His wisdom.

"Plans go wrong for lack of advice; many advisers bring success." (Proverbs 15:22) and "Get all the advice and instruction you can, so you will be wise the rest of your life. (Proverbs 19:20)

Based on scripture, we are to seek advice. In essence, we are to seek out Sams.

But remember, a Sam does not replace a spouse's advice.

"Who can find a virtuous and capable wife? She is more precious than rubies. Her husband can trust her, and she will greatly enrich his life. She brings him good, not harm, all the days of her life." (Proverbs 31:10-12)

A word of caution: be careful in your dealings with various Sams and your spouse. Because there's a pretty good chance you are going to tell your spouse what you're going to do about "X, Y or Z" after listening to your Sam. And your spouse is going to slap you upside the head.

Because that's what they've said all along.

Writing this chapter, I was really nervous showing it to the Little Black Dress. But she got it, so I hope you do.

"There are things that need to be said by your Sam that you just can't accept from your spouse," she said. And that pretty well sums up what I'm trying to say.

More than anyone, I want to celebrate those mountaintop experiences with the Little Black Dress, my wife. And I have. But there's a problem with the mountaintop — that place where you've finally made it. There's only one place to go from there.

When you start tumbling down, and you will, the lucky ones have their own Little Black Dress clearing the trail. It's easy on the top, you'll have plenty of advice up there. But life is brutal on the way down.

CHAPTER FIVE

A SAM WILL WALK WITH YOU TO THE MOUNTAINTOP, YET ALSO THROUGH THE DEEPEST VALLEY

"Lots of people want to ride with you in the limo, but what you want is someone who will take the bus with you when the limo breaks down."
—Oprah Winfrey

"Wealth makes many "friends";
poverty drives them all away."

PROVERBS 19:4

Successful people have friends. They accumulate friends they didn't know were friends. Everyone wants to hang around with successful people.

Put in your cliché — like bees to honey or moths to a flame; successful people never lack company. And that's whether they want them or not. People, by their very nature, are attracted to power, success, and celebrity.

When you're heading up that mountaintop of success, you will not lack for companionship. The saying "it's lonely at the top" is true, but for another reason. There's a big difference between being surrounded by people and being covered by people.

Various people join you on that trip up the mountain — old friends, new friends, and an assortment of others. Many are along for the ride — most just surround you.

Fortunately, there are a few Sams as well, because that's why you're headed up. Never think you did it all by yourself. Someone gave you a loan, a piece of advice, a helping hand, a word of encouragement — those are Sams. Those are the people who cover you.

These types take a different path up that mountain with you. They are usually lagging behind. They have a smile on their face because they relish in your success. Notice I said "your" success; because a true Sam will never take credit.

A Sam will simply say, "I'm glad I could help ... Now go conquer your dragons."

There are times Sams will walk beside you — when you ask. But they will never be in front of you. It's your time. They are pretty humble during your walk. "For those who exalt themselves will be humbled, and those who humble themselves will be exalted" (Luke 14:11) seems to be their mantra.

I quote Proverbs a lot in this book, probably because it's the collected wisdom of the wisest man in the world. It's interesting to note there are 31 chapters — one for each day; although February kind of screws that up. Okay, and those 30-day months, but you get my point.

So you're cruising along enjoying the view on your mountain. And then it happens: you lose your job, someone gets sick, your home burns down, a close friend is killed. You will get slammed by the full force of life and it's not pretty.

And a lot of those friends will disappear. As Proverbs says in chapter 14, "the poor are despised even by their neighbors, while the rich have many 'friends.'"

Your fall is harder because there aren't nearly as many people around to catch you as you tumble. Fact of life: there are a lot more people willing to walk up your mountain than walk down it.

And often that hurts as much as whatever life event you're facing.

David, the second king of Israel, had a special place in God's heart. That's because God had a special place in David's heart. During his long tenure, the warrior-king consolidated Israel into a formidable country.

And he was a heck of a poet. The chapters he wrote in Psalms are some of the most heartfelt, gut-wrenching and intensive prayers you will ever read. And even this great king — a king — watched people turn from him when he was in trouble.

"It is not an enemy who taunts me — I could bear that. It is not my foes who so arrogantly insult me — I could have hidden from them. Instead, it is you — my equal, my companion and close friend. What good fellowship we once enjoyed as we walked together to the house of God." (Psalms 55:12-14)

David was there.

My point is you are not alone. The greatest men in the world have faced the turned back, the whispers, the unanswered phone calls and an empty e-mail box. Been there; didn't like it. I was a newspaper publisher. I ran a news service with a circulation of more than 600,000. When I left, I could count on two hands the number of people who called.

But it is at these low points that real Sams appear. They are the ones who return your calls. They are the ones who simply say, "how can I help?" And then they do. When you are in that deepest valley, just trying to find a single light switch in the darkness, they'll bring a flashlight.

Hopefully your spouse is there alongside you, as well as those close friends. They should be Sams. But there is safety in numbers during these times, you need all the support you can get. It's a war: whether you call it spiritual, mental or physical, you need to get out of that valley.

"So don't go to war without wise guidance; victory depends on having many advisers." (Proverbs 24:6)

During these lowest lows, you need insightful advice and guidance more than ever. And I'd like to say Sams will be jumping out of the woodwork to come help out. That's doubtful. A couple might, but this is when you've got to swallow your pride and find them.

And I can tell you from personal experience that you will. It might be hit or miss for a while, but never give up.

"How can I help?"

In case you missed it, that's the invisible code, the secret handshake, into the fraternal order of Sams. They may only be with you this one time, this one trip out of the valley. Or, they may be around for many more valley excursions.

That's not what matters. What matters is they showed up. Whether you found them or they found you isn't important. What counts is that they were there at your lowest low and darkest deep. Some call it luck, some call it a gift from God.

Make sure you thank them then, and don't forget them when you're back up. "Never let loyalty and kindness leave you! Tie them around your neck as a reminder. Write them deep within your heart." (Proverbs 3:3)

I love these Sams, the ones willing to crawl around in your muck. These are the ones that care more about you than some title. They rank up there with the ones standing by you.

You know the ones. Just you. Your Sams. And your giants.

CHAPTER SIX

A SAM WILL STAND BY YOU EVEN WHEN EVERYONE ELSE HAS DESERTED

"Real friendship is shown in times of trouble;
prosperity is full of friends."
—Euripides

"A friend is always loyal."

PROVERBS 17:17

At one point, he was at the top of the game. Crowds of thousands followed him around for miles, listening to every word he spoke. He was one of the biggest celebrities of his day.

Yet as time wore on and his popularity grew, his message became more pointed. He started making many uncomfortable. He started making some pretty outlandish claims, so much so that many quit believing him.

And he started to make a lot of enemies — the kind you don't want, the ones with all the power. His viewpoints created a huge divide among the people. They either believed him or thought he was crazy; there was little middle ground.

For three years, with a dozen hard-core friends, he pushed his message. It finally became too much for the political and military elite. He was arrested, tried in a fake court and sentenced to death. He went from speaking to thousands to being crucified.

And what of his dozen loyal friends? One betrayed him; at least one we know of actually denied knowing him to others; the others fled after his arrest.

At his lowest low, his best friends left him. Almost.

"When Jesus saw his mother standing there beside the disciple he loved, he said to her, 'Dear woman, here is your son.' and he said to this disciple, 'here is your mother.' And from then on this disciple took her into his home." (John 19:26-27)

Most agree "the disciple he loved" referred to John, one of the original 12 disciples. And he is the only disciple mentioned anywhere in the Bible who was at Jesus' crucifixion.

John was a Sam.

I can't even begin to imagine what all was going through John's mind at the time. It's one thing when your favorite athlete is caught using steroids; or a major politician is found having an affair; or the head of a big corporation is cooking the books.

But this was Jesus, the man John followed for three years as a member of his inner circle. John believed Jesus, believed who he was — the Son of God. And now he watched him being tortured right before his eyes.

Everything John believed about Jesus shattered on that hill history calls Golgotha. Yet he stayed to be beside the one he called "master." He stayed, and later took care of Jesus' mother. I'm sure John was full of doubts, full of fear, but he stayed.

John was a Sam.

There are going to be times in your life when it feels like everyone has deserted you. You stand up after getting slammed by whatever and there's no one around. Let's be honest: there are times when it's not your fault; there are times when it is your fault.

It's your fault if you've broken the law, knowingly insulted others, betrayed a trust, crossed the line. In those instances, you probably are minus those who could help you the most — probably because they are the ones you hurt. There is really only one thing you can do. You must humble yourself, seek forgiveness and do whatever it takes to repair the damage you've done.

And you could really use a Sam right then. Realize this though, a Sam is not going to hold your hand or wipe your tears or find you a snuggle bunny. A true Sam is going to be in your face, demanding you make amends. And they probably won't do anything else until you do.

A person who helps hide your affair, joins in on the backstabbing or closes the bar down with you in commiseration is not a Sam. Those types are not true friends either. They are trouble, and probably part of the reason why you are where you are.

If you are repentant, if you make every effort to fix what you broke, you'll find a Sam. They might end up visiting you in prison, but at least they are there. But you are going to have to take the first step, and the second and probably a third. It takes time. It takes courage.

But sometimes it's not your fault. Your company downsizes or is sold, you lose your job. Your entire retirement fund disappears overnight. I believe some of the quickest ways to see desertion is through the loss of money or position.

Shallow people gravitate to money and to power. And when it's gone, they're gone.

Sams are going to stay around, because they aren't about your money or your title or how you can — or could before the disaster — help them. They are about you. They understand "We all come to the end of our lives as naked and empty-handed as on the day we were born. We can't take our riches with us." (Ecclesiastes 5:15). A similar passage in the New Testament states: "After all, we brought nothing with us when we came into the world, and we can't take anything with us when we leave it." (I Timothy 6:7)

You are more than your money or title or anything the world thinks is important. A Sam gets that. Proverbs 17:17 defines a true Sam: "A friend is always loyal, and a brother is born to help in time of need."

You know the Bible is full of people who at one point lost everything or stood alone against insurmountable odds — guys like Joseph, Job, Ezekiel, Elijah, Elisha, Noah, Jeremiah, Daniel and countless others.

Some were beaten, stoned or whipped. Others were sold into slavery. Some were incredibly wealthy and lost everything they had. A few were betrayed by their closest friends. All were ridiculed publicly, laughed at, despised.

And not one of them did anything wrong. Anyone could understand if they gave up, but for some reason they kept going. They refused to give up even in their darkest despair when all seemed lost.

Why?

They had a Sam. Someone who told them "And be sure of this: I am with you always, even to the end of the age." And they knew that Sam would be there and so they soldiered on.

I'll have more to say about that Sam later.

CHAPTER SEVEN

A SAM WILL SPEAK THE TRUTH IN YOUR LIFE WHEN NO ONE ELSE WILL

"You want answers?"

"I want the truth!"

"You can't handle the truth! ...

You don't want the truth"

—Tom Cruise/Jack Nickolson in *A Few Good Men*

"Those who lead blameless lives and do what is right,

speaking the truth from sincere hearts."

PSALMS 15:2

I was with the same company my entire career. I mean from a couple of months out of college to fast forward nearly a quarter of a century.

The reason I decided to make that phone call isn't relevant to this book. I made it and we'll leave it at that. I began the conversation outlining where I was, what was happening, or not happening, what I was trying to do, what I was …

"John, it's time for you to leave."

That sentence did not come from my boss. It came from a Sam. And I really, really didn't want to hear it. I wanted him to fix it or make it all go away. I wanted him to help me save whatever it was I thought I wanted to save.

What I wanted and what I needed were two separate things. What I needed was for my Sam to say exactly what he did. And I pretty much lost it during that conversation. Twenty-four years with the same company is a long, long time. It was like losing a family.

Not only was it what I needed to hear, it was the right time to hear it. "Timely advice is lovely, like golden apples in a silver basket." (Proverbs 25:11)

A Sam is going to speak the truth in your life even when no one else will and even when you don't necessarily want to hear it. The truth, what you need to hear, is not always fun. Sometimes it hurts. A lot.

The Little Black Dress was praying for me in buckets during that time. So much so I think God at some point just said to her, "yes, I've got him, but how are you?" But she's that way and I am fortunate.

I remember hanging up the phone. I remember looking at her. I remember saying "it's time." I remember her saying "yes it is." And I remember this was late 2008, when our country was in the midst of the worst economic depression since The Great One. Smart move John.

These Sams of Truth rarely bring "tidings of great joy, which shall be for all people." I don't mean they are clouds of doom, it's just truth isn't always easy to hear. But often they are the ones saying "that job isn't right for you," "she's not the one," "it won't be a good fit."

Let's be clear. When you are facing one of those life decisions, a Sam is going to tell it like it is. That might be good; it might be bad. Regardless, realize they have your best interests at heart. They have nothing to gain.

And realize truth is very different from the advice you'll get from anyone you ask. Everyone has an opinion. What you need is honest advice, real truth.

These Sams seem to appear a lot when you're headed down the wrong path. When you, whether you realize it or not, need a course correction.

Peter was one of the original 12 disciples. Not only that, he was part of the inner circle of Jesus, along with James and John. This was the man who was with Jesus from Day One. The one Jesus said he would build his church upon. The man, who after Christ's resurrection, took on any and everyone when it came to proclaiming the Gospel.

Yet at one point, he really needed a Sam.

And one came, from the upstart Paul no less. The same Paul (earlier called Saul) who before his conversion, "was uttering threats with every breath and was eager to kill the Lord's followers" (Acts 9:1). In terms of seniority, Paul had nothing on Peter.

"But when Peter came to Antioch, I (Paul) had to oppose him to his face, for what he did was very wrong." (Galatians 2:11). Wait, what? Mr. Senior "The Rock" Disciple getting rebuked by a newbie? Appears so.

Here's what happened: Peter was eating with some Gentile Christians, but when the Jewish Christians showed up, Peter stopped eating with the Gentiles. You see, there was still some debate amongst the Jews as to whether the Gentiles could really be Christians. And even those Jews who were okay with the whole Gentile Christian thing were still into that separate but equal phase.

It was wrong. Peter was wrong. The Gospel is for all people, regardless of their background. And that's why Paul rebuked Peter. Peter needed a course correction; yes, even the righteous falter every now and then.

We need to celebrate these Sams, even when we're not too crazy about their message. "The king is pleased with words from righteous lips; he loves those who speak honestly." (Proverbs 16:13). And that's what it's about, because in the long run what we need is truth. And that's something the author of Proverbs knew long ago. "In the end, people appreciate honest criticism far more than flattery." (28:23)

The question that you, and only you, must answer is, "can you handle the truth?" That's your call and your decision.

The Little Black Dress is a master in this area. She is the one "speaking the truth in love." She is the perfect guide, but she never leads. Sams never lead.

CHAPTER EIGHT

A SAM IS A GUIDE, NOT A LEADER

"Other people may be there to help us, teach us, guide us along our path, but the lesson to be learned is always ours."

—Unknown

"You guide me with your counsel, leading me to a glorious destiny."

PSALMS 73:24

There is a subtle difference between the words "lead" and "guide."

A leader, by definition, is one "who leads or guides," while a guide is one "who shows the way by leading, directing, or advising." In a real sense, a leader is one who is in charge; a guide is one who lights the path, showing the way.

Sams are guides. They can lead in the sense of guiding, but they should never lead as in being in command of your life. You are ultimately in control of your own destiny. You are ultimately responsible for your decisions and your actions.

If you rely on another individual to make your decisions you are essentially empowering that person to take over. Your life is no longer your own. You are making that person your crutch.

A Sam is not a crutch.

Let's face it, there are times we'd like to just give up and have someone else make our decisions. We've hit our wall. Potential employers aren't returning phone calls; you got turned down for that job you thought was yours; you've got the mortgage payment coming up; your health insurance is running out.

You are facing all of the above and much more. I've faced all that and more. I remember a time when the governor and his wife would come over for dinner; where I would meet every week with the state Senate president, state Speaker and other high ranking politicians.

I remember being unemployed for more than a year.

You want to talk about giving up? It is almost impossible to explain the emotional roller coaster one goes through from being at the top of their game to standing in line for unemployment.

I didn't want any more advice. I wanted to find some genie in the bottle and have unlimited wishes. Nothing worked, nothing was happening.

You may not be where I was, but wherever you are in life, there are going to be times when you need guidance. Thinking about a career change, an investment, the 16-gig or 32-gig iPhone? You need some help.

Hello Sam.

Time after time the Bible tells us to seek counsel, to seek advice. And that's not just some direction for the everyday Joe; some of the greatest leaders in the Bible sought advice.

Moses was one. This was the guy who grew up in Egypt as a prince, who spent 40 years in the wilderness, who came back to Egypt and took on Pharaoh. This was a guy who delivered the 10 plagues, who split the Red Sea, who led an entire nation, who received the Ten Commandments.

This guy: "Inside the Tent of Meeting, the Lord would speak to Moses face to face, as one speaks to a friend." (Exodus 33:11)

Let's just think about that for a moment. Here's Moses, who talks to God like he would talk to a friend. I don't know about you, but that's pretty heady stuff to me. If you're hanging out with God, do you really need any other advice?

But even Moses listened to others. At one point, Moses was basically acting as the judge for every single complaint, accusation, dispute or problem the Israelites had. The Bible says "they waited on him from morning to evening." (Exodus 18:13)

And out of the blue comes Moses' father-in-law, who basically told Moses he was crazy to try and do everything himself, "You're going to wear yourself out—and the people, too," the Bible says. His father-in-law, Jethro, told Moses to appoint other elders to help out with the day-to-day decisions and for him to focus on the "big stuff."

"Moses listened to his father-in-law's advice and followed his suggestions." (Exodus 18:24)

If someone with the background and leadership abilities of Moses can take guidance from others, so can you. Even if it does turn out to be your father-in-law.

Centuries earlier, another man needed help. At the time, the Pharaoh of Egypt was probably the most powerful person in the world. Yet he was troubled by some dreams he couldn't understand. The Bible says he was "very disturbed by the dreams."

So Pharaoh summons all his advisers and wise men. Unfortunately for them, they couldn't figure out what the dreams meant. Finally, someone suggested Pharaoh ask a guy named Joseph, a Hebrew who was sold into slavery in Egypt and whose current address was prison.

The short version: Joseph interpreted the dreams and told Pharaoh not only what would happen (a famine), but what to do (start storing food). "Joseph's suggestions were well received by Pharaoh and his officials," the Bible says in Genesis 41:37.

There are some interesting parallels in these two men. Both were powerful leaders. Both faced problems they couldn't resolve. Both sought guidance. Both listened. And while not implicit, I'd guess they both mulled it over for a while. The Bible doesn't say whether Moses talked to anyone else about his father-in-law's suggestion, but it's quite clear Pharaoh discussed Joseph's proposals with his other advisers.

I want to emphasize again that these two men sought counsel and listened. We need to seek guidance; we need to listen. That is not to say we just take the advice of the first person we find. We need to seek out honest advice, we need to seek guidance from those with no ulterior motives, with nothing to gain.

And the more the better. Because you'll find after a while that real Sams — your Sams — seem to gel together in their suggestions. There may be a few variations, but the majority of the time, the majority of them will be guiding you along the same path.

"Plans go wrong for lack of advice; many advisers bring success." (Proverbs 15:22)

My dad is a Sam, to me and to countless others. My dad is wicked smart, seriously one of the smartest business people I know. And I've heard on more than one occasion the "well, you should really get your dad's advice on that" from way too many people.

Sometimes that's hard, seeking advice from your dad or whatever father-figure you have in your life. We want to succeed on our own. We, you, can't. My dad is retired, yet I'll still go seek his guidance. He always kids around that "well, you're going to get what you pay for." But I know deep down he has my best interests at heart.

I know that because he tells me. More importantly, he shows it. I don't always take his advice, but over the last few years he has never once said "well I told you to do this." When we talk now, my dad is very clear to emphasize that the decision is mine. What he offers is his opinion, his guidance, based on the facts as he sees them.

Sams are guides. Yet even the best guides sometimes miss the path. You see Sams have their limitations — they're just like you.

CHAPTER NINE

SAMS ARE HUMAN

"A mere friend will agree with you,
but a real friend will argue."
—Russian Proverb

*"Indeed, we all make many mistakes. For if we could
control our tongues, we would be perfect and
could also control ourselves in every other way."*
JAMES 3:2

Several years ago I was offered a transfer to another
division within my company. The division was four
times as large with more than twice as many employ-
ees. In the eyes of everyone, this was a promotion.

I wasn't so sure this was the right path for me. So I
sought the advice of as many people as I could — people

who understood the situation and who could give me good counsel. Every one of them encouraged me to take the job.

I did. Looking back, it was the wrong decision. In my gut, or spirit if you will, I always had reservations. Yet all my Sams thought it was the right call. And I listened to them. Were they wrong? In one sense, no. The transfer made sense. If I was someone's advisor in this case, I would have given the same counsel. But in hindsight, it was just the wrong move for me.

I was never really happy there. Yet despite that, fortunately I met another Sam there. He truly was a mentor and counselor. To this day, I know I can pick up the phone and he will tell me like it is and do whatever he can to help. He was one who "spoke the truth," to the point of encouraging me to take yet another position within the company. And he was my boss at the time.

This chapter is a reality check. Life would be a lot easier if we could just find our Sams, take their advice and conquer the world.

It's not that simple. As I said earlier, Sams are not angels or cosmic saviors. They are far from perfect. They have their own stuff; they have their own issues and problems. Think of it this way, Sams are just like you.

I want to be clear. I'm talking about real Sams, not about the guy who lied to you, the one who tried to get the upper hand, who betrayed you, who let you down. Those people aren't Sams.

A Sam is only as good as the information you give them. They don't have the whole story — they have what you tell them. Their observations and advice are based on what they are given and what they have observed and absorbed on their own life journey.

The more information you give these individuals, the better they can help you. The question you have to face is how open are you going to be with your Sams? That's not an easy thing to do, especially for guys. That baring of your soul, your hurts and fears, isn't as easy as writing this sentence.

In other chapters I talk about how Sams are not a crutch and that they can only do so much. And, again, they are human. They make mistakes; their advice might just be flat out wrong. In Ecclesiastes, the Bible says "no one really knows what is going to happen; no one can predict the future." (10:14)

What is important to focus on, however, is the intent. Sams are going to give you what they believe to be the best advice based on what they know. Their intent is to help. But Sams are not perfect and it is flat out wrong to treat **a** Sam like some wise oracle on top of the mountain. Notice the emphasis.

I believe that's one reason why the Bible stresses getting advice from as many people as possible. The following verses highlight that fact. (Emphases are mine)

"Plans go wrong for lack of advice; **many advisers** bring success." (Proverbs 15:22)

"Get **all** the advice and instruction you can, so you will be wise the rest of your life (Proverbs 19:20)

"Without wise leadership, a nation falls; there is safety in having **many advisers**." (Proverbs 11:14)

"So don't go to war without wise guidance; victory depends on having **many advisers**" (Proverbs 24:6)

I hope you get the point. There are countless stories throughout the Bible of Very Important People, some definitely not godly, who surrounded themselves with many advisers — The Egyptian Pharaoh, kings of Assyria, Babylon, and Persia.

"Get all," have "many." Over and over again. I wish I could say I followed that advice in my career. I didn't always and paid for it. The best decisions I made always included the advice of many; poor decisions I made on my own, or relied on someone who told me what I wanted to hear.

But I learned. I'm slowly developing my own mantra regarding advice: *"I already know what I want to hear and I already know what I think. Tell me <u>what you think</u>."* And the more people I ask that, the better chance I have to make the right decision.

Rarely is one decision perfect. Usually, there are pros and cons, strengths and weaknesses of any option. That's why Sams are so important in times like this. Each one looks at a situation differently; each one has their own attributes and expertise. And in reality, that's a good thing.

We need differing points of view. We need the various strengths these individuals bring to the table. The Bible states: "In his grace, God has given us different gifts for doing certain things well." (Romans 12:6)

Sams are not always going to agree. That does not mean that one is necessarily right and another wrong. They view through their own life lens; their own experiences. That's why, as mentioned earlier, the more the better.

I can recall numerous times in my life where I've sought advice from people I trusted; people I knew were men of integrity. Joe will tell me one thing; Bill tells me just the opposite. Great, now what?

For me, I listened to the various viewpoints. Each had its own merits. And I was fortunate in knowing that each of those men had my best interests at heart. They just had different perspectives. You take what you are given and, as we'll see in another chapter, weigh it and make the decision.

It is absolutely imperative you seek individuals of integrity. Men of, to use a word that is sadly losing its place in society, honor. The advice you seek will be as good — or bad — as the people from whom you seek it. "The words of the godly are a life-giving fountain; the words of the wicked conceal violent intentions," the Bible says. (Proverbs 10:11). And it's repeated time and time again, even a couple of chapters later in Proverbs 12:5: "The plans of the godly are just; the advice of the wicked is treacherous."

Before we close this chapter, let's deal with what is commonly referred to as the "elephant in the room."

Sams are human. They are going to make mistakes. And sometimes, they are going to let you down, at least in your eyes. But there are times when they just have their own issues they are trying to handle and they don't — or can't — have time for you.

At the absolutely lowest point in my career, when I faced the biggest decision ever, I reached out to a very specific Sam. This was about as close to an "ultimate Sam" as you can get. He guided me throughout my professional life; he was an incredible counselor, adviser and encourager.

I called. He did not return the call. I called again. No dice. I was crushed.

This man was my last hope. This time, however, he did not take my calls. And I was certain he knew what I needed. It was a horrible time for both of us — he was going through his own stuff at the time. It was all inter-connected. Despite that painful life lesson, he remains someone I still greatly respect — true Sams have that kind of impact.

Sams are human. Despite my encouragement about seeking them out, you must remember they are just like you. They have their own issues and they are human, thus flawed.

Your life is yours; it cannot be led by a Sam.

Why?

Because in the end, it's up to you.

CHAPTER TEN

IN THE END,
IT'S UP TO YOU

"In the end, there can be only one"
—Christopher Lambert (Connor MacLeod),
The Highlander

"This is my command — be strong and courageous!
Do not be afraid or discouraged. For the Lord
your God is with you wherever you go."

JOSHUA 1:9

A Sam can only do so much.

A true Sam loves walking up the mountaintop with you, but will bear down and tumble with you down into the deepest valley. They will speak the truth into your life. They will guard your back, sometimes your front. A Sam is loyal.

A Sam is all this and more. But in the end, it's up to you.

We can gather our Sams, face our demons and charge. We are surrounded by those whose only interest is our best interest. Those who, for whatever reason, took us under their wings and led us to this point. Those who have guided, advised and strengthened us throughout our journey. Bring it on!

I wish. Because there is that invisible line in life. The one no Sam can cross. Even if they wanted to, they can't. You will turn around, look at them and say "come on." And they will be standing there, looking at you. They will slowly shake their heads, and simply say "good luck."

In the end, it's up to you.

At first, it almost feels like betrayal. These Sams have stood by you since you found them, or they found you. The time has come, the decision to fight is now. And that's exactly the point — the decision is now, and only you can make it.

A Sam can carry you; a Sam cannot carry your burden. Whether it be a job decision, whom to marry, what school to go to, whether to buy this or that house, the decision is ultimately, and only, yours.

I wish it was easier. It's not. Only you can pull the trigger or take the bullet out. No one can do either for you. And I know it's probably not what you want to hear; I don't like hearing it either. There is no option. And, you are going to have to live with that decision. Those decisions have consequences.

As I mentioned earlier, I was with the same company my entire professional life — 24 years. It was, to use the old expression, time to fish or cut bait. I sought the counsel of everyone I possibly could, I tried everything I could to see if I could fix the issue. I was incredibly blessed to get advice from people whose primary focus was me and my welfare.

Yet in the end, I had to make the decision. Everyone does. You do.

Despite all the straight talk so far in this chapter, the future reality is better. Because after you've made your decision and gotten your breath back, it's time to look up. You'll be happy you did.

Your Sams are going to be right there beside you. You did what you thought best, meditating on their counsel. Now, they're ready to move along with you. And they are ready to see you through, in whatever capacity you need. The kicker: those Sams will include some whose opinion you didn't take. Maybe they said left, you went right. It doesn't matter. They understand that ultimately, you are responsible. Their job was to provide advice on the impacts for whatever path you chose. Now, they are eager to help you clear that trail you selected.

That's a Sam.

Your decision may not be popular; some might think it was crazy. Sort of like leaving your job after 24 years in the worst economy ever with no prospects lined up. But your Sams, the real ones, are going to be there. The Little Black Dress was always there.

"How can I help?"

You'll still hear that line. Be thankful for it. If you're like me, you'll need to hear it even more after your decision, because now the real work begins. That's okay, you'll still need those people in your life to guide you on your new path.

It is a lonely time. Sitting at the kitchen table, taking that walk or the long drive in the car as you clear your mind and focus. But if you have sought out Sams, realize they are there. You might not see them, but they are doing what they can.

That's exactly what happened in *The King Returns,* the final movie of the Lord of the Rings trilogy. Two events are happening simultaneously. The hero, Frodo, and his sidekick Sam are sneaking their way into Mordor to Mount Doom where the lake of fire is located. Frodo must throw the ring of power he has carried throughout the saga into the lake to destroy it. Doing so will destroy the power of Sauron, the evil lord.

At the same time, the remaining heroes, Aragorn (the future king), Gandalf (the powerful wizard) Legolas (the elf) and Gimli (the dwarf) have just defeated Sauron's forces at the battle of Gondor. It is a temporary reprieve, because Sauron is massing a far greater force to attack again. All the while, Sauron continues to use his powerful, searching eye to find the ring.

The heroes of Gondor can no longer help Frodo. His quest is his alone, the decision is his alone to make. All appears lost, evil will take over Middle Earth. Or will it?

Aragorn and his friends make a fateful decision. They cannot reach Frodo to help him, but they have another option. Gathering their meager forces, already decimated and weakened from the last battle, they head straight for Mordor.

It's a diversion. Their goal is to attack, forcing Sauron to focus on them and give up his search for Frodo. And so with their handful of troops, they call out Sauron and his 300,000 orcs for battle.

Their tactic works, giving Frodo and Sam the time they need to destroy the ring. Exactly how the ring is destroyed we'll leave to the movie.

The point is that each of those standing at the gates of Mordor were Sams. They could not take the path with Frodo, but they did what they could to help him. There, in the background, those warriors stood by Frodo, although not literally.

Although your Sams may not be beside you, remember you are not alone.

"A person standing alone can be attacked and defeated, but two can stand back-to-back and conquer. Three are even better, for a triple-braided cord is not easily broken." (Ecclesiastes 4:12)

So far in this book we've talked about Sams, who and what they are and are not. Now it's time to go find them.

CHAPTER ELEVEN

LOOKING FOR A SAM

"Some people go to priests;
others to poetry; I to my friends."
—Virginia Woolf

"Keep on asking, and you will receive what you ask for. Keep on seeking, and you will find. Keep on knocking, and the door will be opened to you."

MATTHEW 7:7

There is no listing in the Yellow Pages for "The Royal and Ancient Order of the Fellowship of Sams." You're not going to find anything under the "services offered" section of the newspaper either. Sorry.

You need to look. And there's nothing in the Sam Book of Order that says it's an easy journey. There is no secret formula, no special incantation and no runes you must decipher.

Pick up the phone; sit down across from someone. "I need some advice" is a pretty good start. Real Sams are more than willing to help out. But you really, really need to ask for help. They are not clairvoyant.

You also need to be sincere in your request. "And even when you ask, you don't get it because your motives are all wrong — you want only what will give you pleasure." (James 4:3)

If you need help, you need to ask, you need to be truthful and you need to be as explicit as possible. You are wasting your time and a potential Sam's time if he has to turn to you and ask you "what exactly is it you want from me?" Go in with a clear vision, a clear need and ask away.

The Bible often refers to advice or counsel as "wisdom." And throughout the scriptures we are encouraged (some would say, commanded) to seek wisdom. Those who "despise wisdom and discipline" are called "fools" in scripture.

But the Bible is clear: "Tune your ears to wisdom, and concentrate on understanding. Cry out for insight, and ask for understanding. Search for them as you would for silver; seek them like hidden treasures." (Proverbs 2:2-4)

I don't know about you, but I get the sense scriptures are talking about taking a pretty pro-active role, like looking for treasure. We're not talking about lifting up the sofa cushion and finding some loose change. We're talking about that Very Important Meeting you have and you absolutely must leave right now because your entire career depends on being on time and ... You can't find your car keys.

Does the word "frantic" come to mind? Picture yourself in that situation and tell me how you would search.

Go back over the above scripture again. "Tune" or listen; "concentrate;" "cry out;" "ask;" "search." I'd say those words describe a very active role on your part. And that's what you need to do — ask, look, seek and listen.

By taking those initiatives, you're going to find Sams. More importantly, the Bible says that "wisdom is sweet to your soul. If you find it, you will have a bright future, and your hopes will not be cut short." (Proverbs 24:14). If that's not clear enough, "How much better to get wisdom than gold, and good judgment than silver!" (Proverbs 16:16). And this was written by whom the Bible calls the wisest man ever. As in then or now.

I would encourage you to get out of your comfort zone. Asking the people you always hang around with isn't always the best plan of attack. Don't you already know what they're going to say anyway?

Instead, seek out those who've walked a similar journey. Those who've faced similar situations; those who are smarter than you. "Fools think their own way is right, but the wise listen to others." (Proverbs 12:15)

You are looking for a Sam, so look for those with integrity, those who have knowledge in whatever issue it is you are facing. The quality of the advice you get is in direct proportion to the quality of the person giving it.

There's an old tale from Aesop's Fables called "The Ass and His Purchaser." In a nutshell:

"A man wished to purchase an ass and decided to give the animal a test before buying him. He took the ass home and put him in the field with his other asses.

"The new ass strayed from the others to join the one that was the laziest and the biggest eater of them all.

"Seeing this, the man led him back to his owner. When the owner asked how he could have tested the

ass in such a short time, the man answered, 'I didn't even need to see how he worked. I knew he would be just like the one he chose to be his friend.'"

Choose your Sams wisely.

There is a flip side. Sometimes you get lucky. A Sam pops into your life. Why? I don't know, but many would say it's from God, not luck. But for whatever reason, they just seem to show up. You'll know them because they serve as a check in your gut — usually right before you're about to do something really stupid.

I've had those — Sams who just happened to call or I bumped into at just the right moment. It usually starts with my describing something I'm about to do. There will be this pause, and then my Sam will say something along the lines of "Oh really?" followed by "You might want to think about that for a minute."

When you hear that, stop. There's a Sam willing to impart some wisdom in your life.

There are a lot of these types that just seem to appear in the Bible at very specific times. The angels who whisked Lot and his family out of Sodom; a Hebrew slave who saved Egypt from famine; a girl who saved her entire nation; angels who freed Peter from prison. That's just a sampling.

Earlier I said Sams aren't angels. Based on the above examples, yes, sometimes they are. But the vast majority of times they aren't. You never know. What is important is not what the Sam is, what matters is the Sam is there.

So whatever your experience, please make sure you do one thing — listen. "Come and listen to my counsel. I'll share my heart with you and make you wise." (Proverbs 1:23)

I encourage you to seek out your Sams. Never give up. I'd also suggest you look in a very specific place, somewhere you might not have considered yet. That's because Sams are human, disregarding an angel here or there.

Earlier I told you about a man who was as close to an "ultimate Sam" as you could get. And how I thought he wasn't there when I needed him the most.

Now, I'd like to introduce you to the true, "Ultimate Sam."

CHAPTER TWELVE

THE ULTIMATE SAM

"Don't walk in front of me, I may not follow;
Don't walk behind me, I may not lead;
Walk beside me, and just be my friend."
—Albert Camus

*"And be sure of this: I am with you always,
even to the end of the age."*
MATTHEW 28:20

It was decision time.

Earlier in the evening, he ate dinner with his closest friends. He tried to explain what was about to happen, the decision he was facing. They didn't really get it. In fact, they were pretty adamant he was wrong.

After dinner, they headed up to one of their favorite spots, a grove of olive trees. He took his three closest friends a little deeper into the grove, asking them to wait there for him. He needed to think; he needed to pray.

He came back a little later. All three were asleep. He woke them up, talked to them briefly and went off alone again. His decision was weighing heavily on his mind. He went back to his three friends again. And again, they were asleep. He left them there and went back to his thoughts.

When he returned the third time, same deal. "Go ahead and sleep," he said. "Have your rest. But look — the time has come."

He made his decision.

The above story is taken from Matthew, the first book in the New Testament. It's about a man named Jesus and his three closest friends — men named Peter, James and John. I'd like to say those three were Jesus' Sams. That they advised and counseled Jesus; that they stood by him on the mountaintop and in the deepest valley; that they were there at Jesus' darkest time.

On that point they were. Sort of. But they slept while Jesus made the most agonizing decision anyone could ever face. You really can't fault Peter, James and John for dropping the Sam ball when Jesus needed them the most. In the end, it was Jesus' decision, and his decision alone. And as I said before, they didn't really get it.

They didn't really get who Jesus was. They didn't really get — right then at least — that Jesus not only had a direct connection with the Ultimate Sam; that Jesus also was the Ultimate Sam.

Jesus had friends while he was on earth. But He only had one Sam — his Father, God. Master and creator of the universe.

The Ultimate Sam: God the Father; God the Son; God the Holy Spirit — three in one. The perfect Sam.

I'll be the first to admit the whole Trinity thing is a little difficult to wrap your head around. The idea that God, Jesus and the Holy Spirit are each separate and distinct; yet also one. I also can't really wrap my head around gravity; I know what it is and what it does. Explaining it is another thing.

Some things you just have to accept on faith.

We try to complicate Christianity. It really boils down to a few "yes" or "no" questions. God is God. Or He's not. Jesus is the Son of God. Or He's not. The Bible is the living word of God and thus infallible. Or it's not. The only way to have eternal life is by accepting Jesus as your personal lord and savior. Or it's not.

There are no "yeah, buts."

If you answered yes to those four questions, you can tap into the Perfect, the Ultimate Sam. Time and time again the Bible — God's word — promises you the greatest Sam possible. A Sam who will stand with you forever, "even to the end of the age."

But as I said in an earlier chapter, in the end, it's up to you. The choice is yours and yours alone.

When Jesus returned to heaven, He was replaced by the third part of the Trinity — the Holy Spirit; also known as "the Spirit of Truth." When we accept Jesus into our lives, this great adviser enters our hearts. What more could you ask for?

We are told in Galatians to "let the Holy Spirit guide your lives." Elsewhere, we are told in Romans that the "Holy Spirit helps us in our weakness." The Holy Spirit is referred to as our advocate, our counselor, as in "But when the Father sends the Advocate as my representative — that is, the Holy Spirit — he will teach you everything and will remind you of everything I have told you." (John 14:26). It is the Holy Spirit, as John writes in his gospel, "who leads into all truth."

Just like with a human Sam, you still need to do your part. You have to ask. "Keep on asking, and you will receive what you ask for. Keep on seeking, and you will find. Keep on knocking, and the door will be opened to you." (Matthew 7:7) Notice the repetition: "keep" on asking; "keep" on seeking; "keep" on knocking.

In other words, don't give up.

The choice is yours. You can tie your life and all your decisions to the greatest Sam possible. You can rely on God, who has promised to take care of you, has promised to never leave you. Or, you can try it your way. And how is that working out for you?

It's your choice.

Oh, and that decision Jesus made while his friends slept? He decided He would die for you. He decided He would give up his Godness, separate Himself from His Father and take all sin — then, now and in the future — upon Himself as the ultimate sacrifice.

And why? So that through faith in Him, you can — and will — experience eternal life.

Jesus differs from Sam in the Lord of the Rings. If you recall, Sam and Frodo are trying to get up Mount Doom to throw the ring of power into the lake of fire to destroy it. Doing so will destroy the evil lord Sauron. Frodo is done, exhausted. He can't take another step.

And then Sam says, "Come, Mr. Frodo. I can't carry it for you, but I can carry you."

Jesus is saying, "Come. I can carry it for you … and I can carry you."

And that, my friends, is the Ultimate Sam.

CHAPTER THIRTEEN

FINAL THOUGHTS

Sams are a gift of God. He brings them into our lives in His timing. The key is whether we will recognize them and heed their counsel.

Sams have covered my life. Several of them took the time out to read or edit this book. Their advice always strengthened the final product.

Sometimes Sams point out the obvious. And because it's obvious, we miss it. Earlier I talked about the Trinity, how God is distinct yet made up of three. In essence, God's very being — his makeup — is that of a Sam. Even God is not alone. It's God the Father, God the Son and God the Holy Spirit.

A Sam showed me that.

Another Sam pointed out something else. Sams stay with you a lifetime, even after they have passed on. True Sams leave a lasting impression — their counsel, advice and guidance, if heeded, can carry you through a lifetime.

And while death eventually takes our Sams, one will always remain.

God wants to be your Ultimate Sam. And my prayer is you will tap into the Perfect, Ultimate Sam.

He also wants to use you. He wants to use you to change the world, even if it's only one person at a time.

Do you want to change the world? Then do it.

Be a Sam.

PART TWO

SAMS ON SAMS

Earlier in this book I talked about the Sams in my life. Those individuals who stood by me, gave me guidance or just helped steer me down the right path.

I can never repay them.

But I will try.

It is said one should never start a list thanking people, because sure as the world, you are going to leave someone out. I'm going to leave a lot out. It's not that I want to, it's just there is not enough paper in the world.

Nevertheless, on the following pages you are going to meet some of my Sams. These are individuals who represent various points in my life. Some of them were there for a period of time, others are still around.

Let's just call this a sampling, so to speak, of the countless Sams who positively impacted my life. I asked these individuals to recount a time when they had their own Sam, and what they learned from them.

Following are their stories.

You see, even Sams have Sams.

CHAPTER FOURTEEN

SAMS ON SAMS

OTIS WINTERS

Everyone who chooses a career in business needs someone to help them navigate the unknown shoals.

I was a naive young man starting a new company and tended to believe everything I was told. Fortunately, a wise man crossed my path. He was the senior partner of a regional accounting firm and became the Chairman of my Board of Directors.

He was approximately the same age as my father and like most young men, I found it easier to talk to him than my dad. As a professional accountant he had seen many situations, people and companies. He was the perfect counselor for me and helped me on many occasions. One in particular, however, stands out.

One day I had become very upset with one of our suppliers because I thought their sales vice president had reneged on a verbal commitment he had given me about the price of a critical component. He said I had misunderstood what he said.

I went to my mentor, torn between anger and disappointment, to seek his advice before I called a lawyer. Once again his wisdom and experience taught me two great business principles for the price of one visit.

First, he said, "be careful how you listen because too often you hear what you want to hear." Second, "always commit your agreements to paper as quickly as possible."

But, I said, "that means the other party does not trust me and I always do what I say because my word is my bond."

"It may be," my chairman said, "but written agreements between gentlemen merely remind them of what they said."

I knew instantly he was right and perhaps I had misunderstood what had been said. It is important to have mentors, but even better to learn from them.

DENNIS SODOMKA

Art Levin was my high school English teacher and newspaper adviser. My 8th grade English teacher was his wife and she steered me to him.

I learned a lot about writing, editing and leading from him, but the biggest lesson was one I didn't want to learn: you can't do everything; you have to make choices.

I love sports, especially football and baseball, and played two years in high school while working on the student weekly newspaper. Several times Mr. Levin reminded me that if I were serious about journalism I'd have to give up sports. He said I needed to have a goal and always keep it in mind.

Reluctantly, I gave up sports. And I had more great memories in newspapers than I could ever recount.

I talked to him about a year ago, and he remembered my love of sports and asked if I regretted choosing the newspaper. I said absolutely not, and that I was glad he forced me to make the choice.

I've known Gregory Favre for about 35 years, and as great a newsman as he is, I'm grateful to him for showing me it's OK to be friends with people who work for you. You can have fun and be in a serious business.

When he was the managing editor of the Chicago Daily News, no one worked harder. He could be a tough editor, yet we had some great racquet ball matches. And when we found ourselves with Chicago Bears season tickets a row apart, he and his wife Bea would bring the hot buttered rum to games.

I didn't realize it until later, but I actually learned a lot of journalism during those social occasions. Gregory also loves to cook and often had staff members over for dinner, or brought food into the office.

I've talked to other people who worked for him in other cities and they all tell the same stories about how much they learned from Gregory at those informal gatherings. He also stood up for me and showed me how to pick my way through the minefield of a merged newsroom when the Daily News died and some of us were moved to the morning Sun-Times. Through the years whenever I needed help sorting through a tough problem I could always count on Gregory for solid advice.

ANNA FALLING

One spring day my dad introduced me to a friend of his who was building his own airplane. I was 12 at the time.

For some reason, I got it in my head that I sure would like to fly that little two-seater airplane. Sure enough, not too long afterward the plane was ready to fly and my dad made arrangements for me to take a ride.

After an exhilarating afternoon in the clouds, flying over the rivers and hills of Oklahoma's Indian country, I was hooked. And I daydreamed, seeing myself flying my own plane over the snow-covered valleys, hopping from city to city saving the world.

A few years later my family and I moved from our small town to the big city of Tulsa, where there were bigger airplanes and you didn't have to make a preliminary run at the grass landing strip to move the cows off.

My dream was still planted, just a little dormant, until one day I came home from school with a piece of paper announcing a new Explorer Scout session to learn how to fly. I immediately went to my father, ever the Boy Scout, and asked him if this was for girls too.

He responded with a "well, there's only one way to find out …" That night we started the journey to fulfill my dream. By the time I was 16, I had my first solo flight and my pilot's license by the time I was 18.

My dad became my first passenger and we have the moment etched in memory as he exited the plane and promptly kissed the ground. He knew I could fly, he just provided the ways and means to help me soar.

And I knew after that, I could take on the world. At the age of 21, I found myself in China. My dad was my biggest fan, writing faithfully every week on the corner of an aerogramme he shared with my mother.

He cheered and cringed as I filed for public office and surprisingly won. He walked with me down the aisle when I got married; was there when I gave birth to my first child and watched me continue my efforts at saving the world.

But he wasn't surprised by any of this. He just helped me see what he already knew. I could fly.

Sams just know.

DENNY DEWITT

My friend Ron Pavellas has been my mentor since the mid 1970s. We met when he was a hospital administrator in Modesto, California, and I worked for the California Hospital Association.

He provided guidance for about four years to me before moving to Alaska. He encouraged me to apply for the CEO of the Alaska hospital association, which is the job that brought me to Alaska in 1980. Along the way he was chair of my association board and left Alaska about a year before I left to do a stint in Washington DC.

I was divorced in 1984. Ron, who had been divorced, stood by me in some very dark and discouraging days during that time. His willingness to share his experiences helped me believe that there was a light at the end of the tunnel.

Later the next year my job became very tenuous and Ron was a great help in managing the situation. Several years later, Ron was himself looking for a job and I was able to help him land a position in Homer, Alaska. Ron has retired and moved to Sweden. We stay in touch through email and Facebook. He just wrote a letter of recommendation for me and I just finished briefing a friend of his on long term care in America.

At one time when my character was challenged, I remember Ron looking across the table and saying quietly and firmly, "I trust Denny with my life, this discussion is finished." That statement very much helped me, but it also forced me to listen to Ron when he made suggestions I didn't want to hear. There was never any question that he had my best interests in mind.

JULIAN MILLER

My "Sam" was actually a "Bill", W. S. "Billy" Morris III, to be exact. He was the CEO of the company and he loved to tell me I was not a publisher any more than he was a CEO. "We are nothing but teachers," he would say, "Our jobs are to help others grow. Hopefully, we will be better next year than we are this year."

His teaching experiences were many and varied.

In the 1980s, Billy owned not only the second largest newspaper in the state, but the largest locally owned company in Augusta, Georgia. He was pretty much depended on for everything in the community and he contributed to all, but got little credit for it. One day the Augusta Rowing Regatta came calling, asking how to make the nationwide collegiate competition on the Savannah River more successful.

They really wanted a contribution. But they asked for advice, and Billy was trying to give it.

After a quick lunch at a riverside restaurant Billy and the Regatta board, with me in tow, took a hike down the levy that separated the river from

Downtown. It was overgrown, extremely steep and full of flying bugs with teeth near the finish line. Billy immediately saw, "there's no good place to watch the finish." He looked up at a highway bridge overlooking the river and announced, "we need to close the bridge and put bleachers on it."

"Can't," replied a board member. "It's a state highway."

We trekked on for 15 minutes with Billy pausing occasionally to point out the strength of the bridge bleachers, each time getting the same reply. On his fifth mention, he was standing next to me and I foolishly answered, "But you can't close a state highway." Big mistake.

In the time it takes for a mosquito to buzz, Billy had whipped around to face me, our noses inches apart: "Don't tell me what I can't do! People have been doing that all my life. Of course you can close a state highway! It's done all the time. Tell me HOW you're going to get it done."

I never told Billy he couldn't do anything again. And I rarely allowed anyone to tell me, either.

LEON THOMPSON

When I was three years of age my father abandoned my mother and me. Drugs, alcohol and womanizing were the culprit. I never saw my father again until I was 26 years of age. My mother was very young and without support and returned home.

During the years that followed I was raised, for the most part, by my grandparents. My grandmother's heritage was Pennsylvania Dutch Quaker and my grandfather was a New Mexico cowboy. We lived on a small farm in Concord, California, and they both had a great influence in my life. However, the one who had the greatest influence was my Uncle Sam.

My uncle was the youngest of my grandparents' children and was ten years older than I. We shared a room together for over seven years and even to this day we see each other periodically. My uncle was born with cerebral palsy, but had a brilliant mind. He graduated with honors from high school, college, and graduate school with a degree in physics.

Following his formal education he could not find a job. Every interview led to the words: "We'll call you, don't call us." My grandfather, who was not only a farmer but also a builder, saw a discouraged son and decided to teach him carpentry. He would show my Uncle Sam how to lay out a foundation one time and he never forgot it. He began to build houses and never allowed his "handicap" to interfere with his growing abilities in the building trade.

During these years I learned from my uncle to never allow a disability to become a discouragement in life. My uncle began to show me how to nail, cut boards, pour concrete, wire a house, etc. etc. When we weren't building we had chores to accomplish on the farm picking fruit, shelling walnuts and almonds and cultivating the fields. I will always be grateful to a "brother" who taught me so many things in life.

He was also fun and at one time he built a small "roller coaster" in the field. We had more fun riding that dangerous coaster and having several accidents. He took me to the auto races, carnivals, and the circus. When I was twelve years old he taught me how to drive a car. On my sixteenth birthday I was standing at the Department of Motor Vehicles ready to take my driving test.

What I learned from my mentor was a strong foundation in life, which was and still is today, the center of my life. We attended church together and I watched him lead a youth program and teach Sunday school. My uncle was a strong Christian man; and as we shared our room together in those early years I remember his telling me the importance of a foundation in life which would bring meaning, purpose and direction in my life. The foundation was centered on Jesus Christ. I have never forgotten those late night talks, and it is one of the things that led me to become a Presbyterian minister.

It was a sad day when I learned that my uncle was interviewed for a civil service position with the Navy and was hired. This meant that he would be leaving home, which he did. When he began his new job in southern California he soon became a supervisor in the lab where he worked. His specialty was guided missiles. His vocation took him around the world on many occasions. During his years of work with the Navy he continued to build houses in which he lived with his wife and two sons.

We continue to have a brotherly relationship and when his wife died I participated in her funeral service. A few years later he was to marry once again and I participated in the wedding of my new aunt.

People come and go in our lives, but there are those who have a strong influence as our mentors and my Uncle Sam is one of those. We all need an Uncle Sam in our lives.

ROBB KRECKLOW

There have been many changes in classroom education since I left high school in 1969, but I am confident that one thing has remained constant. Good teachers influence students for a lifetime, not just for the year, or less, they have them in a classroom.

That's how I felt after learning that Cecil M. Richmond had passed away in my Nebraska hometown. He was 90 years old.

You don't know him, of course, but I hope you know someone like him. Mister Richmond, as nearly everyone in the school and the community called him, was that special teacher, who taught me the value of lifelong learning.

Our relationship began in the late spring of 1967 as I was registering for classes for my junior year. Mr. Richmond taught English composition and literature to juniors. He ran a disciplined classroom, using a half dozen different texts. Most students and many teachers felt he resided over one of the most challenging classrooms at Beatrice High School, chemistry and pre-calculus being the other two.

Owing to the faulty recommendation of a junior high school teacher, I had been removed from the college preparatory track as I entered my sophomore year. I told my guidance counselor I wanted back into the program, and I wanted to register for Mr. Richmond's class.

My guidance counselor balked, and I went to see Mr. Richmond. And yes, I was scared to death. I still remember how Mr. Richmond sat me down in front of his desk and grilled me.

He did not ask me to name the eight parts of speech. He did not ask me to conjugate a single verb. He did not ask me who had won the Nobel Prize in Literature for 1938. (Pearl Buck) He asked me what I wanted to do with my life. He asked me what plans I had for reaching my goals. He challenged me to ask him questions about the class.

In other words, we had a literate conversation. After about 20 minutes, he motioned for me to follow him. We walked quietly through the hallways to the counselor's office, where he told my adviser to place me in his class.

You see, Mr. Richmond did not just teach English. He used the English curriculum to teach life skills, including, but not limited to, critical thinking, writing, and public speaking.

Along the way, he created a passion for excellence and a love for learning. Even in retirement 24 years ago, he taught me yet another lesson. Cecil Richmond retired to something, not from something.

He became one of the most respected and appreciated stage performers in community theater and he remained active at his church, where he was a longtime Sunday School teacher and choir director.

He also continued his active participation in Rotary International and the local retired teacher's group. I feel guilty that I never told him directly how much he meant to me and to many of my fellow classmates. I suspect he knew full well.

I always visited with him at Rotary Club meetings, during my trips home. If ever there was a man for all seasons, Cecil Richmond was that man. I am better for having spent nine months in his classroom — or should I say 37 years in his shadow.

Educational administrators and school boards can cast as many programs as they like on a student body. However, nothing succeeds better than a teacher who can create in students a lifetime of curiosity and a passion for learning. Cecil Richmond was such a teacher.

SUZANNE YACK

I had this publisher once. He was new at his job, I was new at mine. I had two kids in middle school and probably bit off more than I could chew stepping up to run the newsroom during a tectonic shift in management.

Now my publisher was young, ambitious, smart and occasionally brash, and he set standards for conduct. His ethical approach to news was admirable — he came from the news side of the business. I can't even remember what it was I did that got me called into his office one day. He was never shy about calling things like they were. I probably let some story go through without having it fairly told from both sides. A snarky headline or perhaps something I said out in the community that made its way back to him.

It's not important the offense, although I recall it was one that could end up in my personnel file. What is important are the words he spoke to me, looking me right in the eyes: "You're better than that."

He didn't say it and glower, nor did I feel crushed with a rebuke. I could tell he cared enough about me to tell me something I needed to hear. Those words have stayed with me since.

Sometimes when I have a mind for revenge or petulance, I am reminded that I'm better than that. They're the wise words that a parent might have said, but no one had ever said those words to me. They were spoken at the right time, when I was able to hear them.

You're better than that. Whatever it is you've done in your life where you didn't measure up to your own standards, remember: You are better than that. My Sam told me that.

Grace gives you right of way to be gentle with yourself about your failings, and Grace gives you the courage to lift up your chin and try again to be a better person than you were just moments before.

Striving for righteousness, mending fences, being kind, focused and capable — these have been some of my own lessons on my journey to being "better than that."

CORBY CARLIN WINTERS
(THE LITTLE BLACK DRESS)

When my husband, John, talked about writing his book *Everyone Needs a Sam*, I could barely contain my enthusiasm. I always believed he had a message and a gift for writing. I was right.

In my own life, I have experienced an abundance of Sams. They came in and out of my life, leaving a lasting impression and changing me forever. I am blessed with many, many Sams, too many to count.

Two of my Sams, however, simply cannot be compared to any others. They rose above the rest and remain held in my highest esteem.

As I was writing this, I was barely able to write through the tears, because again I was reminded of how blessed and fortunate I was to have been guided, loved, and influenced by these two extraordinary people.

The Sams I want to honor are my Mother and Father. To me they epitomized and embodied the meaning of a Sam. Hardly a day does not go by that I do not recount a wise word that was passed on to me by them. Hopefully, the author will forgive me for choosing two Sams. It is impossible to select one because their impact on me was equally strong.

I always knew I was in a privileged circle because I was in the presence of these Sams from the beginning and through my journey of life. They were not perfect, but they were amazing. I credit them for the woman I am today.

I was given the privilege to know how Sams work and operate firsthand. They poured into the lives of those around them for no selfish reasons but to simply bless, encourage and empower others.

I believe all my friends knew my parents were Sams too. Everyone wanted to come to our house. My Sams had open arms and hearts. Friends sought my parent's prayers, advice and support for their futures, and I was no exception. My Sams prayed for and led many of my friends and my brother's friends to the Lord. Strangers were no exception from their special touch either.

My earliest remembrances of my parents were those of encouragement, support and faith in me and my abilities. Having been diagnosed with dyslexia and a learning disability in third grade, it shaped how I viewed myself and the world around me. Most of my educational experience was a struggle. In turn, it made me insecure and I lacked self confidence. But my parents knew what to do and did it just right.

My mom steered me toward what I excelled in, such as public speaking, singing, art and acting. I remember asking her how I would ever get a job when I couldn't even spell and was horrible in math. Her reply was "you'll hire a secretary"! Well she was right. Every job I ever had, I had a secretary. Then I married a writer and editor ... you gotta love it!

One time my mom mailed me my third grade report card. It was filled with D and F's. I called her and asked why she mailed it to me, because it seemed odd to remind me of such a difficult time. Mom said "she wanted me to see how far I had come, Master's Degree and all"

To help me with my confidence, my mom enrolled me in modeling and charm schools. At the time of my first fashion show, when I was about 11, I panicked. I just couldn't go through with it. I remember my dad calling from work and saying "You have worked hard and now you have what it takes to finish what you started. If you don't want to do another one after this that is fine, but you will want to finish this one. You are prepared and you can do it."

I did finish and loved every minute of it. He was so right. I remember it as though it was yesterday. That kind of wisdom — finish what you start — has stayed with me all these years.

When I was starting a small business back about five years ago, Daddy sent me a small handwritten note dated 9/5/05. It read: "Success is the result of: **1.** Having a dream **2.** Give it all you've got **3.** Believe in yourself and believe in your dream **4.** Work within your limits and your capabilities **5.** Enjoy and love what you are doing **6.** Set some realistic goals for yourself and be patient. Enjoy! Love Mom and Dad."

I have a box filled with notes of inspiration just like that one. They never held back an opportunity to encourage, to teach and to love.

What a gift it was for me to have my parents as Sams; they were my favorite ones. They spoke life and purpose into my life. But most of all, they spoke the love of Jesus Christ to me and everyone they met. They gave me all the tools anyone could ever ask for to help them succeed.

And now in the words of my husband, I encourage you, be a Sam!

PART THREE

CHAPTER FIFTEEN

YOUR STORY

And so we come to the end; or maybe the next step.

Everyone needs a Sam. And everyone has Sams in their life. We need to celebrate these individuals; we need to thank them; we need to remember what they taught us.

To that end, we have set up a web site where you can write about the Sam or Sams in your own life. We hope you will share your story; not only to recognize them, but so others can learn the wisdom of your own Sams.

This is your chance.

Please visit http://everyoneneedsasam.com and tell the world your story.

> *"As iron sharpens iron,*
> *so a friend sharpens a friend."*
>
> PROVERBS 27:17